Learn SAP Concur: A Guide to Streamline Expense and Travel Management

Table of Contents:

Chapter 1: Introduction to SAP Concur

Welcome to Chapter 1 of "Mastering SAP Concur: A Comprehensive Guide to Streamline Expense and Travel Management." In this chapter, we will provide you with an introduction to SAP Concur, its benefits, and an overview of its key features and modules.

Section 1.1: What is SAP Concur?

SAP Concur is a leading cloud-based platform that helps organizations streamline their expense and travel management processes. It offers a comprehensive suite of solutions that enable businesses to simplify expense reporting, automate travel booking, enforce policy compliance, and gain valuable insights through analytics.

Section 1.2: Benefits of using SAP Concur

SAP Concur offers several benefits that can greatly enhance your expense and travel management practices. Some of the key advantages include:

Efficiency and Time Savings: SAP Concur automates manual processes, such as expense reporting and travel booking, reducing the time and effort required to manage these tasks. This frees up valuable time for employees and allows them to focus on more strategic activities.

Policy Compliance: With SAP Concur, you can configure expense policies and rules, ensuring that employees adhere to company guidelines. This helps to prevent non-compliant expenses and reduces the risk of fraud.

Improved Visibility and Control: The platform provides real-time visibility into expenses and travel activities, allowing managers to monitor spending, identify trends, and make data-driven decisions. This visibility helps organizations gain control over their expense management processes.

Integration Capabilities: SAP Concur integrates seamlessly with other systems, such as ERP (Enterprise Resource Planning) solutions, HR systems, and travel partners, enabling data synchronization and streamlining processes across different platforms.

Section 1.3: Key Features and Modules of SAP Concur

SAP Concur consists of various modules that cater to different aspects of expense and travel management. Here are some of the key features and modules:

Expense Management: The expense management module allows users to capture receipts, create expense reports, and submit them for approval. It includes features such as receipt scanning, automatic expense categorization, and policy enforcement.

Travel Booking: SAP Concur's travel booking module provides a user-friendly interface to book flights, hotels, rental cars, and other travel arrangements. It integrates with popular travel partners, ensuring a seamless booking experience.

Policy Configuration: This module allows administrators to define expense policies, configure spending limits, and enforce compliance rules. It ensures that expenses are aligned with company guidelines and regulatory requirements.

Analytics and Reporting: SAP Concur offers robust reporting and analytics capabilities, allowing users to generate expense reports, visualize spending patterns, and extract meaningful insights. Customizable dashboards and templates enable organizations to analyze expense data effectively.

These are just a few of the core features and modules that SAP Concur offers. As you progress through this book, you will learn in-depth about each of these functionalities and how to leverage them effectively.

That concludes Chapter 1, where we introduced you to SAP Concur, its benefits, and its key features and modules. In the next chapter, we will guide you through the process of getting started with SAP Concur, including setting up your account and navigating the platform's interface.

Section 1.4: Target Audience for SAP Concur

SAP Concur caters to a wide range of organizations and individuals involved in expense and travel management. The target audience includes:

Employees: Employees across different departments and roles who incur expenses and need to submit expense reports regularly will benefit from using SAP Concur. Whether they are traveling for business, attending conferences, or making purchases on behalf of the company, SAP Concur simplifies the expense reporting process for them.

Managers and Approvers: Managers responsible for overseeing expense management and approving expense reports will find SAP Concur valuable. It provides them with a centralized platform to review and authorize expenses, ensuring compliance with company policies.

Administrators: System administrators and IT professionals responsible for implementing and maintaining SAP Concur within the organization will benefit from understanding the platform's configuration options, integration capabilities, and security considerations.

Finance and Accounting Professionals: Finance teams involved in expense tracking, budgeting, and financial analysis will find SAP Concur useful. The platform provides them with accurate and up-to-date expense data, enabling them to reconcile accounts, monitor spending patterns, and generate financial reports.

Section 1.5: Prerequisites for Using this Book

To get the most out of this book and effectively learn SAP Concur, it is recommended to have the following prerequisites:

Basic Computer Skills: Familiarity with using computers and web-based applications is essential. Understanding concepts like navigating through web pages, filling out online forms, and working with spreadsheets will be beneficial.

Access to SAP Concur: You will need access to a SAP Concur account or a sandbox environment provided by SAP Concur for practice purposes. If you do not have access, reach out to your organization's administrator or SAP Concur representative to assist you.

Understanding of Expense and Travel Management Processes: A basic understanding of expense and travel management practices within your organization will help you relate to the concepts and functionalities discussed in this book.

Section 1.6: How to Use this Book

This book is designed to be a comprehensive guide to mastering SAP Concur. Each chapter covers specific topics and functionalities, building upon the knowledge gained from the previous chapters. To make the most of this book, consider the following suggestions:

Read the book sequentially: Start from Chapter 1 and progress through the subsequent chapters in order. This will ensure a logical flow of learning and enable you to grasp the concepts effectively.

Practice hands-on: SAP Concur is best learned through hands-on practice. As you encounter practical exercises and examples throughout the book, try to replicate them in your own SAP Concur account or sandbox environment.

Take notes and review: Jot down important concepts, tips, and any questions that arise as you read. Take the time to review your notes periodically to reinforce your understanding.

Engage with the content: Feel free to interact with this book by asking questions or seeking clarification on specific topics.

Understanding SAP Concur thoroughly is our goal, and I am here to assist you along the way.

Congratulations! You have completed the first chapter of "Mastering SAP Concur: A Comprehensive Guide to Streamline Expense and Travel Management." In the next chapter, we will delve into the process of setting up your SAP Concur account and navigating the platform's interface. Let's get started!

Chapter 2: Getting Started with SAP Concur

Welcome to Chapter 2 of "Mastering SAP Concur: A Comprehensive Guide to Streamline Expense and Travel Management." In this chapter, we will walk you through the process of getting started with SAP Concur. We will cover setting up a SAP Concur account, navigating the interface, and understanding user roles and permissions.

Section 2.1: Setting up a SAP Concur Account

To begin using SAP Concur, you need to set up a user account. Follow these steps to create your SAP Concur account:

Contact your organization's SAP Concur administrator or representative: Reach out to the person responsible for managing SAP Concur within your organization. They will provide you with the necessary information and access credentials to create your account.

Access the SAP Concur login page: Open a web browser and go to the SAP Concur login page. The URL is typically provided by your administrator or can be found in your organization's communication.

Click on the "Sign Up" or "Create Account" option: On the login page, look for the option to create a new account. It is usually located below the login form.

Enter your details: Provide the required information, such as your name, email address, and password. Make sure to choose a strong password that meets the specified criteria.

Verify your email: After entering your details, you will receive an email from SAP Concur with a verification link. Click on the link to confirm your email address and complete the account setup process.

Set up your profile: Once your email is verified, you will be prompted to set up your profile. Fill in any necessary personal information, such as your contact details and preferred language.

Configure preferences: SAP Concur allows you to customize certain preferences, such as currency settings, default expense categories, and notification preferences. Take the time to configure these options according to your preferences.

Congratulations! You have successfully created your SAP
Concur account. Now, let's explore the SAP Concur interface.

Section 2.2: Navigating the SAP Concur Interface

The SAP Concur interface is designed to provide a user-
friendly and intuitive experience. Here are some key
elements and sections you will encounter:

Dashboard: The dashboard serves as the main landing page
after you log in. It provides an overview of your pending
tasks, recent expense activities, and important notifications.
The dashboard can be customized to display relevant widgets
and reports.

Navigation Menu: The navigation menu is located either on
the left-hand side or at the top of the screen, depending on
the configuration. It allows you to access different modules
and functionalities within SAP Concur, such as Expense,
Travel, Approvals, Reports, and Settings.

Expense Module: The Expense module is where you create,
manage, and submit expense reports. It provides options to
add expenses, attach receipts, categorize expenses, and

review policy compliance. You can also track the status of your submitted expense reports from this section.

Travel Module: The Travel module is used for booking and managing travel arrangements. It allows you to search for flights, hotels, rental cars, and other travel services. You can view itineraries, make bookings, and access travel-related information and assistance.

Approvals: The Approvals section is where you can review and approve expense reports, travel requests, and other pending items. This section is typically accessible to managers and approvers within the organization.

Reports and Analytics: The Reports section provides various reporting and analytics tools to generate expense reports, view spending trends, and extract insights. You can customize reports, apply filters, and export data for further analysis.

Section 2.3: User Roles and Permissions

SAP Concur utilizes a role-based access control system to manage user permissions and ensure data security. Here are some common user roles you may encounter:

Employee: An employee role typically has the ability to create and submit expense reports, book travel, and view their own expense history. They may also have access to certain reporting and analytics features based on their organization's configuration.

Manager/Approver: Managers or approvers have additional permissions to review and approve expense reports, travel requests, and other pending items from their team members. They may also have access to specific reports and analytics related to their team's expenses.

Administrator: Administrators have elevated privileges and are responsible for configuring and maintaining the SAP Concur system within the organization. They can manage user accounts, set up expense policies, configure integrations, and perform system maintenance tasks.

Note: User roles and permissions may vary depending on your organization's specific configuration and requirements. It's important to consult your SAP Concur administrator or representative to understand the roles and permissions assigned to you.

Congratulations! You have now learned how to set up a SAP Concur account, navigate the interface, and understand user roles and permissions. In the next chapter, we will dive into the process of managing expenses with SAP Concur, including capturing receipts, creating expense reports, and submitting them for approval. Let's continue our journey to master SAP Concur!

Chapter 3: Managing Expenses

Welcome to Chapter 3 of "Mastering SAP Concur: A Comprehensive Guide to Streamline Expense and Travel Management." In this chapter, we will explore the process of managing expenses with SAP Concur. We will cover how to capture receipts, create expense reports, and submit them for approval.

Section 3.1: Capturing Receipts

Capturing and attaching receipts to your expense reports is a crucial step in ensuring accurate and compliant expense tracking. SAP Concur provides multiple methods for capturing receipts:

Receipt Scanning: With the SAP Concur mobile app, you can easily capture receipts by using your smartphone's camera. Open the app, navigate to the Expense module, and select the option to capture a receipt. Align the receipt within the camera frame and take a photo. The app will automatically extract relevant details from the receipt, such as merchant name, date, and amount.

Email Receipts: If you receive receipts via email, you can forward them to a designated SAP Concur email address. The system will process the email and extract receipt data for future expense matching.

File Upload: If you have digital copies of your receipts, you can directly upload them to SAP Concur. In the Expense module, navigate to the expense entry and select the option to attach a receipt. Choose the file from your computer or device and upload it.

Smart Receipt Capture: SAP Concur offers Smart Receipt Capture powered by machine learning. When creating an expense entry, simply enter the merchant name and total amount. SAP Concur will attempt to match the transaction with an existing receipt in its database, automatically populating the relevant details.

Section 3.2: Creating Expense Reports

Once you have captured your receipts, it's time to create expense reports. Here's how you can do it in SAP Concur:

Navigate to the Expense module: Log in to SAP Concur and go to the Expense module using the navigation menu.

Add Expenses: Click on the "New Expense" or "Add Expense" button to start creating a new expense entry. Fill in the required details, such as the expense date, merchant, amount, and expense category. You can also attach the corresponding receipt using the methods mentioned in Section 3.1.

Categorize Expenses: Assign appropriate expense categories to each entry to help with tracking and reporting. SAP Concur provides predefined expense categories, but you can also customize them to match your organization's needs.

Review Policy Compliance: SAP Concur automatically checks each expense entry against your organization's expense policies. It highlights any policy violations or warnings, such as excessive spending or missing receipts. Review these alerts and make necessary adjustments to ensure compliance.

Add Additional Details: Depending on your organization's requirements, you may need to provide additional information for certain expenses. This could include project codes, cost centers, or client names. Fill in these details as needed.

Save and Continue: Save each expense entry as you add them. SAP Concur allows you to save your progress and continue working on the report at a later time.

Section 3.3: Submitting Expense Reports for Approval

Once you have added all the necessary expenses to your report, it's time to submit it for approval. Follow these steps to submit your expense report:

Review Expense Entries: Before submitting, take a moment to review all the expenses in your report. Ensure that everything is accurate, receipts are attached, and compliance warnings are addressed.

Submit for Approval: Click on the "Submit" or "Send for Approval" button to initiate the submission process. SAP Concur will prompt you to select the appropriate approver(s) for your report. Choose the correct approver based on your organization's approval workflow.

Add Comments (if necessary): If you need to provide any additional context or explanations to the approver, you can include comments along with your expense report submission.

Submit and Await Approval: Once you have completed the submission, your expense report will be sent to the designated approver(s) for review. You can track the status of your report in the SAP Concur system.

Congratulations! You have learned how to capture receipts, create expense entries, and submit expense reports in SAP Concur. In the next chapter, we will explore the travel management capabilities of SAP Concur, including booking travel arrangements and managing itineraries. Let's continue our journey to master SAP Concur!

Chapter 4: Travel Management

Welcome to Chapter 4 of "Mastering SAP Concur: A Comprehensive Guide to Streamline Expense and Travel Management." In this chapter, we will delve into the travel management capabilities of SAP Concur. We will cover how to book and manage travel reservations, integrate with travel partners, and utilize the mobile app for on-the-go travel management.

Section 4.1: Booking Travel Reservations

SAP Concur provides a user-friendly interface for booking and managing travel arrangements. Here's how you can book travel using SAP Concur:

Navigate to the Travel module: Log in to SAP Concur and access the Travel module from the navigation menu.

Search for Travel Options: Within the Travel module, you can search for flights, hotels, rental cars, and other travel services. Enter your travel details, such as the destination, dates, and preferences.

Compare and Select Options: SAP Concur will present you with a list of available options based on your search criteria. Compare prices, schedules, and other relevant details to make an informed decision.

Make a Booking: Once you have selected your preferred option, click on "Book" or "Select." Follow the prompts to provide necessary traveler information, such as passenger names, loyalty program numbers, and any special requirements.

Review and Confirm: Before finalizing the booking, review all the details to ensure accuracy. Check the itinerary, travel dates, and pricing information. If everything looks correct, proceed to confirm the booking.

Receive Confirmation: After confirming the booking, you will receive a confirmation email or notification containing the booking details and itinerary. The information will also be stored in your SAP Concur account for easy reference.

Section 4.2: Integrating with Travel Partners and Airlines

SAP Concur offers seamless integration with travel partners and airlines, allowing for a smoother travel booking experience. Here's how integration works:

Configure Travel Preferences: Within SAP Concur, you can configure your travel preferences, such as airline preferences, hotel chains, and car rental companies. This ensures that the system presents you with options aligned with your preferences and loyalty programs.

Partner Integration: SAP Concur integrates with various travel partners, such as airlines and hotel chains. This integration allows you to access real-time availability, pricing, and special offers from these partners directly within the SAP Concur system.

Streamlined Booking Process: When booking travel through SAP Concur, the system automatically communicates with the integrated travel partners. This streamlines the booking process and eliminates the need to visit multiple websites or platforms.

Loyalty Program Integration: SAP Concur can sync with your loyalty program accounts, allowing you to earn points, track rewards, and access member benefits seamlessly. Make sure to link your loyalty program accounts within your SAP Concur profile.

Section 4.3: Mobile Travel Management with SAP Concur App

SAP Concur offers a mobile app that enables on-the-go travel management. Here's how you can utilize the mobile app:

Download and Install the App: Search for the SAP Concur app in your device's app store (available for iOS and Android). Download and install the app on your smartphone or tablet.

Login and Sync: Open the app and log in using your SAP Concur credentials. The app will sync with your SAP Concur account, retrieving your travel itineraries and expense data.

Access Travel Itineraries: Use the app to view your travel itineraries, including flight details, hotel reservations, and car rentals. The app provides easy access to important travel information, such as confirmation numbers, directions, and contact details.

Mobile Booking: The SAP Concur app allows you to search and book travel arrangements directly from your mobile device. You can search for flights, hotels, and rental cars, and complete the booking process within the app.

Expense Capture on the Go: The app also provides the functionality to capture and upload receipts while traveling. Use the receipt scanning feature to capture receipts, categorize expenses, and attach them to your expense entries.

Travel Notifications and Alerts: The app keeps you informed about flight delays, gate changes, and other travel-related updates. It sends notifications and alerts to ensure you stay informed and can adjust your plans accordingly.

Congratulations! You have learned how to book travel reservations, integrate with travel partners, and utilize the SAP Concur mobile app for on-the-go travel management. In the next chapter, we will dive into expense compliance and policy enforcement within SAP Concur. Let's continue our journey to master SAP Concur!

Chapter 5: Expense Compliance and Policy Enforcement

Welcome to Chapter 5 of "Mastering SAP Concur: A Comprehensive Guide to Streamline Expense and Travel Management." In this chapter, we will explore how SAP Concur helps organizations ensure expense compliance and enforce policy guidelines. We will cover configuring expense policies, monitoring and auditing expenses, and handling policy violations.

Section 5.1: Configuring Expense Policies and Guidelines

Configuring expense policies and guidelines is essential for maintaining expense compliance within an organization. SAP Concur provides a flexible framework to define and enforce these policies. Here's how you can configure expense policies in SAP Concur:

Access Policy Configuration: As an administrator, log in to SAP Concur and navigate to the Policy Configuration section. This area allows you to define and customize expense policies according to your organization's requirements.

Create Expense Categories: Start by creating expense categories that align with your organization's expense structure. Define categories such as meals, transportation, accommodation, and entertainment.

Set Spending Limits: Assign spending limits to each expense category or to specific employees or departments. These limits help control expenses and prevent overspending.

Define Policy Rules: Specify policy rules for each expense category, such as maximum allowable amounts, acceptable vendors, or restrictions on certain expenses. These rules ensure that expenses adhere to company guidelines.

Receipt Requirements: Determine the receipt requirements for different types of expenses. Specify when receipts are mandatory, and set thresholds for when receipts can be waived.

Policy Violation Actions: Define actions and notifications for policy violations. Determine how violations are flagged, who is notified, and the appropriate steps for resolving non-compliant expenses.

Section 5.2: Enforcing Expense Compliance

SAP Concur provides tools to monitor and enforce expense compliance within your organization. Here's how you can enforce expense compliance using SAP Concur:

Real-Time Policy Checking: SAP Concur automatically checks expense entries against configured policies in real-time. When an employee submits an expense report, the system verifies the entries for compliance with policy rules and alerts them to any violations or warnings.

Compliance Warnings and Notifications: SAP Concur notifies employees and managers about compliance warnings or policy violations. These notifications provide an opportunity to address issues and ensure that expenses align with company guidelines.

Manager Review and Approval: Managers or designated approvers play a crucial role in enforcing expense compliance. They review expense reports, validate expenses against policies, and provide necessary approvals or rejections based on compliance considerations.

Exception Handling: SAP Concur allows for exceptions to policy rules, such as business-related justifications or special circumstances. Administrators can define exception processes and provide guidelines for managing exceptions effectively.

Section 5.3: Monitoring and Auditing Expenses

Monitoring and auditing expenses help ensure ongoing compliance and detect any potential issues. SAP Concur provides features to facilitate monitoring and auditing processes. Here's how you can monitor and audit expenses using SAP Concur:

Reporting and Analytics: Utilize SAP Concur's reporting and analytics capabilities to generate expense reports, identify spending patterns, and gain insights into expense management. Customize reports to focus on specific expense categories, departments, or time periods.

Audit Trails: SAP Concur maintains detailed audit trails of expense activities, providing a transparent view of expense history. These trails capture information such as expense creation, modification, approval, and reimbursement details.

Periodic Audits: Conduct periodic audits of expenses to ensure compliance and identify potential issues. Utilize SAP Concur's reporting features to analyze expense data, flag unusual spending patterns, and investigate anomalies.

Compliance Reporting: Leverage SAP Concur's compliance reporting tools to track policy adherence, monitor violations, and generate compliance-related reports. These reports provide visibility into compliance metrics and help identify areas for improvement.

Section 5.4: Handling Policy Violations

Occasionally, policy violations may occur within an organization. SAP Concur provides mechanisms to handle policy violations effectively. Here's how you can handle policy violations using SAP Concur:

Exception Management: SAP Concur allows you to define exception processes for handling policy violations. Determine how exceptions are reviewed, approved, and documented. Set guidelines for employees to provide justifications for non-compliant expenses.

Manager Escalation: In cases where policy violations require further review or escalation, SAP Concur enables managers to escalate the issue to appropriate authorities or the finance department. This ensures proper handling of policy violations and resolution.

Policy Education and Communication: Communicate expense policies and guidelines effectively within your organization. Regularly educate employees on policy requirements, provide training on SAP Concur usage, and address any questions or concerns related to expense compliance.

Congratulations! You have learned how to configure expense policies, enforce compliance, monitor and audit expenses, and handle policy violations using SAP Concur. In the next chapter, we will explore reporting and analytics features in SAP Concur, allowing you to gain valuable insights from your expense data. Let's continue our journey to master SAP Concur!

Chapter 6: Reporting and Analytics

Welcome to Chapter 6 of "Mastering SAP Concur: A Comprehensive Guide to Streamline Expense and Travel Management." In this chapter, we will explore the reporting and analytics capabilities of SAP Concur. We will cover how to generate expense reports, analyze expense data, customize reports, and share insights with stakeholders.

Section 6.1: Generating Expense Reports

SAP Concur provides robust reporting features to generate expense reports. Here's how you can generate expense reports using SAP Concur:

Navigate to the Reports section: Log in to SAP Concur and access the Reports section from the navigation menu.

Select Report Type: Choose the type of report you want to generate. SAP Concur offers various pre-built report templates, such as expense summary reports, detailed expense reports, and mileage reports.

Customize Report Parameters: Specify the report parameters, such as the date range, expense categories, departments, and any other relevant filters. These parameters allow you to focus the report on specific criteria.

Generate the Report: Click on the "Generate" or "Run Report" button to generate the report based on the selected parameters. SAP Concur will process the data and generate the report in the desired format.

Review and Validate the Report: Once the report is generated, review it to ensure accuracy and completeness. Validate that the expense data and details align with your expectations.

Export or Save the Report: SAP Concur allows you to export the report in various formats, such as PDF, Excel, or CSV. Choose the appropriate format based on your requirements. You can also save the report within SAP Concur for future reference.

Section 6.2: Analyzing Expense Data and Trends

SAP Concur's reporting and analytics capabilities enable you to analyze expense data and identify spending trends. Here's how you can analyze expense data using SAP Concur:

Utilize Pre-Built Dashboards: SAP Concur offers pre-built dashboards that provide visual representations of expense data. These dashboards present key metrics, charts, and graphs to help you understand spending patterns at a glance.

Apply Filters and Drill-Down: Customize your analysis by applying filters and drill-down capabilities. Filter the data based on criteria such as departments, expense categories, or specific time periods. Drill down into specific expense entries for more granular analysis.

Identify Spending Trends: Analyze expense data to identify spending trends and patterns. Look for insights such as the most frequent expense categories, top spending areas, or any outliers that may require attention.

Compare Periods: Compare expense data across different time periods to observe changes and trends. Analyze year-over-year or month-over-month comparisons to identify any significant shifts in spending.

Section 6.3: Customizing Reports and Creating Templates

SAP Concur allows you to customize reports and create templates tailored to your organization's requirements. Here's how you can customize reports and create templates using SAP Concur:

Report Customization Options: SAP Concur provides options to customize the appearance and content of reports. Customize elements such as headers, footers, fonts, and color schemes to match your organization's branding.

Add Custom Fields: SAP Concur allows you to add custom fields to reports. These fields can capture additional information or specific data points that are relevant to your organization's reporting needs.

Save Customizations as Templates: Once you have customized a report to your satisfaction, save it as a template for future use. Saved templates enable you to generate consistent reports with your preferred configurations.

Share Report Templates: SAP Concur allows you to share report templates with other users within your organization. This promotes consistency in reporting and allows stakeholders to access predefined templates for their analysis.

Section 6.4: Exporting and Sharing Expense Reports

SAP Concur offers options to export and share expense reports with stakeholders. Here's how you can export and share expense reports using SAP Concur:

Export Report Data: Within SAP Concur, you can export reports in various formats, such as PDF, Excel, or CSV. Choose the appropriate format based on the intended use or sharing requirements.

Email Reports: SAP Concur allows you to email reports directly from the system. Select the report you want to share, specify the recipients, and include any necessary comments or instructions.

Share Reports via URL: Instead of emailing reports, you can generate a shareable URL for the report. This URL can be shared with stakeholders, granting them access to the report without the need for email attachments.

Schedule Report Distribution: SAP Concur allows you to schedule automated report distribution. Define the recipients, frequency, and format of the reports to be delivered automatically at specified intervals.

Congratulations! You have learned how to generate expense reports, analyze expense data, customize reports, and share insights using SAP Concur. In the next chapter, we will explore integration and automation options within SAP Concur, allowing you to streamline processes and enhance productivity. Let's continue our journey to master SAP Concur!

Chapter 7: Integration and Automation

Welcome to Chapter 7 of "Mastering SAP Concur: A Comprehensive Guide to Streamline Expense and Travel Management." In this chapter, we will explore integration and automation options within SAP Concur. We will cover how to integrate SAP Concur with other systems, configure data synchronization, automate expense and travel processes, and utilize APIs for custom integrations.

Section 7.1: Integrating SAP Concur with Other Systems

SAP Concur offers integration capabilities to connect with other systems within your organization. Integration streamlines data exchange, reduces manual effort, and improves overall efficiency. Here's how you can integrate SAP Concur with other systems:

ERP System Integration: SAP Concur can be integrated with your organization's ERP (Enterprise Resource Planning) system. This integration enables seamless data synchronization between SAP Concur and your ERP system, ensuring consistent financial reporting and streamlined processes.

HR System Integration: Integrating SAP Concur with your HR system allows for automatic synchronization of employee information. This integration ensures that employee details, such as names, departments, and cost centers, are up to date within SAP Concur.

Travel Partner Integration: SAP Concur integrates with various travel partners, such as airlines, hotel chains, and car rental agencies. This integration provides real-time availability, pricing, and booking capabilities directly within SAP Concur, eliminating the need for manual data entry or navigating multiple platforms.

Credit Card Integration: By integrating SAP Concur with corporate credit card providers, you can automate the process of importing credit card transactions into expense reports. This integration ensures accurate and efficient expense reconciliation.

Section 7.2: Configuring Data Integration and Synchronization

Configuring data integration and synchronization is essential to ensure accurate and up-to-date information within SAP Concur. Here's how you can configure data integration and synchronization:

Data Mapping: Determine the mapping between data fields in SAP Concur and the connected systems. Identify corresponding fields for employee information, expense categories, cost centers, and other relevant data elements.

Schedule Data Sync: Define the frequency and schedule for data synchronization between SAP Concur and the connected systems. Determine when and how often data updates should occur to maintain data consistency.

Validate and Test: Before deploying data integration, thoroughly test the synchronization process to ensure data accuracy and integrity. Validate that the data is transferred correctly and matches the expected outcomes.

Monitor and Troubleshoot: Continuously monitor the data integration process to identify any issues or discrepancies. Implement mechanisms to track data synchronization errors and perform necessary troubleshooting steps.

Section 7.3: Automating Expense and Travel Processes

SAP Concur offers automation capabilities to streamline expense and travel processes, reducing manual effort and improving efficiency. Here's how you can automate processes using SAP Concur:

Expense Report Auto-Population: SAP Concur can automatically populate expense reports with relevant data, such as credit card transactions or travel itineraries. This automation eliminates the need for manual data entry, saving time and reducing errors.

Expense Approval Workflows: Configure automated approval workflows within SAP Concur to streamline the approval process. Set up rules and criteria for different approval levels, ensuring that expense reports are routed to the appropriate approvers automatically.

Expense Reimbursement Automation: Automate the reimbursement process by integrating SAP Concur with your organization's payroll or finance system. This integration enables direct deposit of reimbursements, eliminating the need for manual checks and reducing processing time.

Travel Booking Automation: Utilize SAP Concur's travel booking capabilities and preferences to automate the process of booking flights, hotels, and rental cars. Implement rules and configurations to ensure compliance with travel policies while providing employees with convenient booking options.

Section 7.4: Using APIs for Custom Integrations

SAP Concur provides APIs (Application Programming Interfaces) that allow for custom integrations and extended functionality. APIs enable developers to interact with SAP Concur and build custom solutions. Here's how you can utilize APIs within SAP Concur:

Explore the SAP Concur API Documentation: Access the SAP Concur API documentation to understand the available APIs, their functionalities, and how to use them. Familiarize yourself with the API endpoints, request formats, and authentication methods.

Identify Integration Opportunities: Determine areas where custom integrations can enhance your expense and travel management processes. Identify tasks or systems that can be connected with SAP Concur through custom API integrations.

Develop Custom Solutions: Engage with your development team or utilize external developers to build custom solutions using the SAP Concur APIs. Leverage the APIs to extend the capabilities of SAP Concur and tailor the platform to your organization's specific needs.

Test and Deploy: Thoroughly test the custom integrations to ensure functionality, data accuracy, and security. Once the integrations are tested and validated, deploy them in your production environment.

Congratulations! You have learned how to integrate SAP Concur with other systems, configure data integration and synchronization, automate expense and travel processes, and utilize APIs for custom integrations. In the next chapter, we will explore best practices for implementing SAP Concur within your organization and maximizing its benefits. Let's continue our journey to master SAP Concur!

Chapter 8: Best Practices for SAP Concur Implementation

Welcome to Chapter 8 of "Mastering SAP Concur: A Comprehensive Guide to Streamline Expense and Travel Management." In this chapter, we will explore best practices for implementing SAP Concur within your organization. These practices will help you maximize the benefits of SAP Concur and ensure a successful implementation.

Section 8.1: Establish Clear Objectives

Before implementing SAP Concur, it's crucial to establish clear objectives for the project. Define the specific goals and outcomes you want to achieve with SAP Concur, such as streamlining expense reporting, improving policy compliance, or enhancing travel management. Having clear objectives will guide your implementation strategy and ensure alignment with your organization's needs.

Section 8.2: Involve Key Stakeholders

Ensure that key stakeholders are involved throughout the implementation process. This includes representatives from finance, HR, IT, travel management, and other relevant departments. Collaborate with these stakeholders to gather requirements, define processes, and ensure that SAP Concur meets their needs. Engaging stakeholders from the beginning fosters ownership and buy-in, increasing the likelihood of a successful implementation.

Section 8.3: Customize Configuration to Fit Your Organization

Take advantage of the customization options in SAP Concur to align the system with your organization's specific requirements. Customize expense categories, policy rules, approval workflows, and other settings to reflect your organization's structure and processes. Tailoring SAP Concur to your organization's needs will maximize user adoption and improve efficiency.

Section 8.4: Provide Comprehensive Training

Invest in comprehensive training for employees who will be using SAP Concur. Offer training sessions, workshops, or online tutorials to familiarize users with the system's functionalities, processes, and best practices. Ensure that employees understand how to capture expenses, submit reports, book travel, and adhere to policy guidelines.

Ongoing training and support will foster confidence and proficiency among users.

Section 8.5: Communicate Benefits and Expectations

Communicate the benefits of SAP Concur to your employees and stakeholders. Highlight how the system will streamline processes, improve efficiency, and enhance their experience. Clearly communicate the expectations for using SAP Concur, such as timely submission of expense reports, adherence to policy guidelines, and participation in training activities. Transparent communication will promote user engagement and commitment.

Section 8.6: Conduct a Pilot Phase

Consider conducting a pilot phase before rolling out SAP Concur organization-wide. Select a group of users or a specific department to participate in the pilot phase. Gather feedback, identify any issues or challenges, and refine your implementation approach based on the pilot results. This iterative approach allows for fine-tuning and ensures a smoother transition to SAP Concur.

Section 8.7: Establish Ongoing Support and Maintenance

After the initial implementation, establish a support structure to address user queries, troubleshoot issues, and provide ongoing assistance. Designate a support team or a point of contact within your organization to handle SAP Concur-related inquiries. Regularly review and update your SAP Concur configuration and policies to align with any organizational changes or evolving requirements.

Section 8.8: Continuously Monitor and Optimize

Regularly monitor the usage, performance, and impact of SAP Concur within your organization. Analyze user feedback, system metrics, and expense data to identify areas for improvement and optimization. Continuously refine your processes, policies, and configuration to maximize the benefits of SAP Concur and drive continuous improvement.

Congratulations! You have learned the best practices for implementing SAP Concur within your organization. By following these practices, you can ensure a successful implementation and unlock the full potential of SAP Concur. In the final chapter, we will summarize key takeaways and provide additional resources to further enhance your SAP

Concur knowledge. Let's conclude our journey to master SAP Concur!

Chapter 9: Summary and Additional Resources

Congratulations on completing "Mastering SAP Concur: A Comprehensive Guide to Streamline Expense and Travel Management!" In this final chapter, let's summarize the key takeaways from our journey and provide additional resources to further enhance your SAP Concur knowledge.

Section 9.1: Key Takeaways

Throughout this guide, you have learned:

How to set up a SAP Concur account, navigate the interface, and understand user roles and permissions.

The process of capturing receipts, creating expense reports, and submitting them for approval.

The travel management capabilities of SAP Concur, including booking travel arrangements and managing itineraries.

The importance of expense compliance and policy enforcement, and how to configure expense policies, monitor expenses, and handle policy violations.

How to generate expense reports, analyze expense data, customize reports, and share insights with stakeholders.

The integration and automation options within SAP Concur, including system integration, data synchronization, process automation, and utilizing APIs for custom integrations.

Best practices for SAP Concur implementation, such as establishing clear objectives, involving key stakeholders, providing comprehensive training, and continuously monitoring and optimizing the system.

Section 9.2: Additional Resources

To further enhance your understanding and proficiency in SAP Concur, consider exploring the following additional resources:

SAP Concur Help Portal: Visit the official SAP Concur Help Portal for comprehensive documentation, user guides, and video tutorials. It provides detailed information on various features and functionalities of SAP Concur.

SAP Concur Community: Join the SAP Concur Community to connect with other SAP Concur users, share experiences, ask questions, and learn from industry experts. The community is a valuable resource for networking and gaining insights into best practices.

Training and Certification: SAP Concur offers training programs and certifications for administrators and users. These programs provide in-depth knowledge and hands-on experience with SAP Concur, validating your expertise.

Webinars and Events: Keep an eye out for webinars and events hosted by SAP Concur. These sessions cover various topics related to expense and travel management, providing opportunities to learn from industry experts and stay updated on the latest trends.

Section 9.3: Conclusion

Congratulations once again on completing "Mastering SAP Concur: A Comprehensive Guide to Streamline Expense and Travel Management." You now have a solid foundation of knowledge to effectively utilize SAP Concur within your organization. Remember to leverage the resources mentioned above and stay connected with the SAP Concur community to further enhance your skills and explore new possibilities.

Wishing you success in your SAP Concur journey and in optimizing your expense and travel management processes. Happy Concurring!

Printed in Great Britain
by Amazon

45611655R00030